"Self-defence is a ... ...elief
that ...

Rorion Graci...
Ulti...

KUNG FU

EVERYONE'S INVITED

8 Smart Self-Defence Techniques
You Must Know

VEDANT J MAHESHWARI

KUNG FU – EVERYONE'S INVITED

First published in 2022 by

Panoma Press Ltd
info@panomapress.com
www.panomapress.com

Book layout by Neil Coe.

978-1-784529-67-3

The right of Vedant J Maheshwari to be identified as the author of this work has been asserted in accordance with sections 77 and 78 of the Copyright, Designs and Patents Act 1988.

A CIP catalogue record for this book is available from the British Library.

All rights reserved. No part of this book may be reproduced in any material form (including photocopying or storing in any medium by electronic means and whether or not transiently or incidentally to some other use of this publication) without the written permission of the copyright holder except in accordance with the provisions of the Copyright, Designs and Patents Act 1988. Applications for the copyright holder's written permission to reproduce any part of this publication should be addressed to the publishers.

This book is available online and in bookstores.

Copyright 2021 Vedant J Maheshwari

ACKNOWLEDGEMENTS

To my *sifus*, Tom and Ollie:

Tom and Ollie are both my Kung Fu *sifus*. They have taught me since I was 11 and built the foundation of my confidence when outside. Both are extremely technically competent at Wing Chun, and if it were not for them, many young children and adults would not know how to defend themselves when necessary.

If you want to learn more advanced techniques and others outside of the ones included in this book, you could even attend weekly Kung Fu classes. Tom and Ollie offer a four-week free trial where you can get accustomed to Kung Fu.

You can book your courses through www.kungfuschoolswimbledon.co.uk

To my parents:

My mother and I spent many hours discussing the issues raised by 'Everyone's Invited', and she helped me become more aware of the current issues at hand and how extensive this problem is. One of the most disturbing things for me was to hear how unsafe she felt when outside. This was a key driver for me to synthesise some key defence techniques that she and others could use and to present them in this book.

My father first introduced me to Kung Fu and martial arts, alongside knowledge on how to be safe in public. Every day, after coming back from Kung Fu class, it would be my father who would help me practise and perfect my techniques. He has also always encouraged me on my Kung Fu journey and continues to do so to this day.

To all my friends who shared their experiences:

I would like to thank everyone who I contacted who shared their experiences of assaults and feeling unsafe around others for helping me understand and appreciate the severity of the matter.

TABLE OF CONTENTS

PREFACE

"I was sitting on the bus in Year 9 coming home from my friend's house. It was dark and in the wintertime. There were no seats left, so I had to sit next to this guy. I was wearing a short dress with tights, and he kept looking at my legs. I tried to ignore him, but he kept watching me. I eventually got off the bus, and he got off and started catcalling me. I ran back home in fear. He wasn't even that old, probably in his late 20s."

"I was groped by different boys at parties. I did not consent to being touched like that, but I felt like if I said I was uncomfortable everyone would ridicule me. It makes me feel sick, and I can't even imagine what it's like for people I know who were raped by boys at the same school."

"When I was 14, I went to a party hosted by a boy. Whilst standing and talking to a friend, one of the boy's friends grabbed me by the waist and pulled me onto his lap. When I tried to get up, he put both arms around my waist and tried to shove his hand down my pants. No one in the room said anything or tried to help me whilst I was struggling to get him off me. When I finally got up and pushed him off his chair, another boy told me I was being a bit harsh and to cut him some slack because he was more drunk than me."

"I was on a date; I was 13, maybe 14, and in middle school. He took me to the movies, and as we sat waiting for the show to start, he started rubbing his hand closer down there and almost trying to unzip me. I did not feel comfortable, and I had only known him for maybe two weeks after my friend had introduced us. He was 17. I kept pushing his hand away and just started coming up with excuses, and thankfully he let it go as we finished the movie. When we were outside leaving, I tried to walk away from him, and he grabbed my hair and pulled it back towards him three times."

These are only four of over 50,000 testimonies on the 'Everyone's Invited' website. Each one of the people giving these testimonies has been sexually assaulted or has felt extremely scared and lacking confidence whilst being alone. At first, it may seem that this issue is not prevalent in society; in fact, I once believed that too. However, there is a high chance that people you know have experienced some sort of sexual assault themselves.

I asked a few friends of mine, who are girls, whether they had experienced any sort of misogyny or rape culture. Keep in mind, I am 15 years old, and they are also around my age. I asked them,

"I'm writing on the topic of 'Everyone's Invited' regarding misogyny and rape culture in daily life. I was wondering if you, yourself, have experienced any rape culture or misogyny (simply even felt scared walking on the streets) or know anyone who has?"

I also followed up with,

"If you were given the opportunity to quickly learn a few martial art moves, would you learn them (to feel more confident on the streets and know that you could protect yourself, if necessary, from any possible threats)?"

For the sake of anonymity, I've changed the names of my friends.

Sara's response:

Sara and I lived in the same area and she used to attend a girls' school around a mile away from our house. My school, a boys' school, is also a few minutes from our house and is on the way to her school. Every day she would have to walk from her school, past my school, to her house. I strongly believe that neither me, nor my friends from school, would ever have acted in misogynistic ways, so I was surprised when I heard what she said to me. This is what I was told,

> "[My school's] boys would yell across the road and catcall my friends and me, so I would wear a coat most of the time so they wouldn't be able to see me fully. I couldn't really do this in the summer, so I just had to put up with what was happening.

> "I remember the utter fear I had when I used to walk past your school every morning and evening.

"I couldn't really do anything about it."

In reply to my second question regarding martial arts, she answered,

"I think anyone would [learn martial art moves] because rape culture isn't just limited to women, it applies to transgender people (these cases are extremely violent and not talked about enough), men, people of colour, people of any gender, the LGBTQ+ community and more."

"I want to be able to feel safe rather than sorry. Hopefully, in the future, things would change so that possible victims can be less worried and not have to use defence mechanisms when in shifty situations, but I think, for now, I wouldn't mind learning a few extra steps towards defending myself because when I used to walk home, especially if it was late, my mum told me not to wear headphones when walking, or to just simply take the bus. My friend who lived on the other side of that alleyway wouldn't take it during the night; she'd have to go all the way around."

My conversations with Sara truly helped me realise the helpless state many girls find themselves in and the confidence many of them may lack to do something about their situation. For some further context, the school I go to is regarded as one of the top schools in London. It is clear to see that regardless of one's upbringing, intellect and education, people can still do horrid things, such as making others feel often uncomfortable. Even though many are taught not to do things like this, they still do.

Maya's response:

Maya is someone I have known since Year 5, when I was nine years old. We used to go to the same school until I left and went to the current school I attend. Later, she moved to a girls' school. This was her reply to my first request,

"Well, personally I have never had any first-hand experience with being assaulted or harassed on the streets, which I'm fortunate enough for, but that certainly doesn't stop me walking home with keys between my fingers or crossing the street if there's someone who looks 'dodgy', which I know is an awful trait for me to judge someone on, but I always feel like I can never be too careful when I'm walking alone. And especially in winter months when it's already dark as soon as school finishes, I used to take a longer journey home just so I could stick to the main roads instead of side streets and I would take busier trains which had more people on them.

"I know some of my friends have been catcalled and provoked in the streets, and I even know a group of very young girls who were walking in broad daylight, facing away from the traffic, when a man tried to force them into the back of his van, which is totally horrifying to think about.

"Even from an early age, being at an only-girls school, we are taught about staying safe on the streets and different products which can enhance our protection or different things we can do in certain situations surrounding rape and assault, which I understand is totally necessary and I am extremely grateful for, yet it's quite alarming that it's such a big issue being experienced by those from such an early age in society."

In reply to the second question, she said,

"Yeah, I definitely would. Having anything to help and protect you on the streets is so important, and I think martial arts especially would be super helpful for so many because once you know it, it's something you can perform at any time and in any situation to defend yourself."

This reply further confirms that many girls feel tremendously uncomfortable on the streets daily knowing that anything may happen.

Tia's response:

Tia is 17, and her brother and I had been going to the same school for quite a few years, and I have known her for a long time since our parents also studied together. She also goes to an only-girls school. In response to my initial question, she said,

"I definitely do not feel safe travelling anywhere alone. I feel like I'm constantly looking around to be aware of my surroundings, and I'm always crossing the road over to the other side when I see strangers walking towards me.

"Even simple things like the fact that every time I'm leaving the house alone my mum feels the need to say, 'Be safe', I think, says a lot.

"A while back, I was on the train coming back from school and I saw a man randomly take a picture of me, which made me feel so uncomfortable and unsafe I just got off the train and walked home instead.

"I have a really close friend who had a boy she knew text her a huge paragraph insulting her and calling her really sexually degrading names just because she didn't reply to a text of his.

"One of my friends was followed by a stranger on the way back from school, and multiple others have told me about being sent sexually explicit images on social media, having had no other interaction with these people online."

In response to my second query, she said,

"Yes, I'd probably like to learn some martial arts moves, but just a personal perspective on this – I feel like learning self-defence for this kind of situation, while important, does make it the responsibility of the victim to defend themselves rather than there being education to stop harassment in the first place. Yes, knowing self-defence would make me feel safe, but knowing that people around me understand consent and respect boundaries would definitely make me feel much safer and more confident on the streets."

To this I replied,

> "I fully agree, and, honestly, that would be ideal. I did mention this in my writing, and the main reason I asked that question is that regardless of how much you teach someone not to do something, such as make others uncomfortable, there is no guarantee they will not do such things. For example, there are masses of intellectuals at my school, yet I know that loads of them catcall people from across the street etc. It's quite a shame really."

Of course, there will always be many girls who have not experienced any forms of sexual assault or misogyny, which is a wonderful thing, but still feel that knowing a martial art would be useful. For example, this is the case with the last friend I asked.

Rose's response:

Rose and I used to go to primary school together. She now goes to an only-girls school. In response to my second question about learning a martial art, she said,

> "I would definitely choose to learn a martial art, but, for me, that's not really got anything to do with rape culture or protecting myself from creepy men. It's something I would have always liked to have been able to do, regardless of what is going on in the world. I think that both girls and boys should be taught self-defence in school as a part of physical education."

The fact that sexual assault cases are ubiquitous is undeniable. Whether it be people you do not know or close friends, it does exist, and something needs to be done about it. At the end of the day, many men, regardless of their situation, are unable to be taught Not to sexually assault people or even not to make them feel uncomfortable.

While this is unfortunate and it in no way makes it the victim's responsibility to defend themselves, there is no guarantee that even with a combination of education and threat of punishment these incidents will reduce to zero.

While a majority of people have never experienced and will hopefully never experience any form of sexual assault or threat, I believe it is vital that everyone should know some basic martial art moves so as to be capable of defending themselves if the time ever comes.

JUST ANOTHER NIGHT

"See you soon…" you say to your friend as she opens the door and steps out into the overwhelming darkness. The echoes of her footsteps slowly recede as they get further away from you. You're the last one at the event, the once-bustling area now deserted and eerily silent. You also move towards the door, turning the cold metal handle and gently tugging at it. A gust of ice-cold air immediately seeps through the opening and floods around you, engulfing you and thrusting you into the outside world, as the door behind you glides back into position.

Everything seems familiar. The refreshing, crisp air filling your lungs, the inordinate quietude only allowing the sound of a singular, distant motorbike to find its way to you alongside the infrequent laughter of a couple walking back home from far away. Everything feels the same as last time you had to walk home alone. What could go wrong… right?

A 20-minute journey is all there is. You begin to walk down the street, looking around at all the shops around you, each hidden behind a veil of gloom and closed signs swung upon their entrances. Everyone is sleeping at home; after all, it is nearly midnight. You turn into a slightly more desolate road; it is the quickest way for you to reach home; the one you always take. As you turn, just from the corner of your eye, you see a figure, draped in black, walking around 100 metres behind you. Of course, without giving it a second thought, you continue down your path, excited to enter the warmth and comfort of your house once again.

You take another turn; again you see the figure still behind you, however, now closer. You notice that this person is moving quite hastily and is approaching you rapidly. You pick up your pace and move swiftly onwards, yet you can now hear the person's footsteps rapidly getting louder and nearer. You can hear their ragged breathing with hints of aggression intertwined between each breath.

"Usually no one else takes this path, let alone at night," you nervously consider to yourself. "Hopefully, this person just passes by."

"Stop," you hear from behind. It is the deep voice of a middle-aged man. You keep moving forward, ignoring the potential threat.

That is when he grabs you tightly by the shoulder and pushes you into a wall by your side, your head colliding painfully against it, leaving you dazed for a few fleeting seconds and unable to comprehend what he is muttering.

The smell of alcohol now lingers in the air around you, storming aside everything pleasant previously felt. He is clearly intoxicated and not thinking straight, but evidently stronger than you. At that very moment, you notice his hand reach out towards you.

If only there was a simple, effective way to know what may be coming next and how to defend yourself against it. This book has been written to help in situations like this.

IS IT REALLY THAT BAD?

Sure, being attacked on the streets is a possibility; but is the probability really that high? To understand the extent and severity of this issue, let us focus and talk about the concentrated topic of sexual assault in England and Wales itself. Around 97,000 adults, from the ages of 16–59, experience some sort of attempted rape or sexual assault here every year. At first, this number may not seem to be a profusion in comparison to these two countries' populations of around 56 million. However, if we further explore the statistic of 97,000 cases per 365 days, within a brief period we would realise this number equates to there being 11 sexual assaults every hour! And this in a forward-thinking developed country like the UK.

Keep in mind that this is not including violent attacks or robbery. And this is an ongoing issue which does not seem to be going away. How long has this been going on for? Why am I bringing attention to this concern now?

The wide-scale social awareness of this issue began in the 1970s when the term 'rape culture' was coined in the United States by second-wave feminists. Rape culture is a sociological theory in which rape and sexual assault are prevalent as well as normalised due to societal attitudes regarding sexuality and gender. Behaviour associated with rape culture includes actions such as slut-shaming, the objectification of people, the trivialisation of rape and even refusing to acknowledge the harm caused by sexual assault. Before the introduction of the term rape culture in the United States in the 1970s, most Americans believed that rape, incest and female domestic abuse were infrequent. It was further discovered that rape was considered to be something normal rather than immoral in American culture and was a manifestation of societal sexism and misogyny.

Frankly, rape culture affects nearly every woman. Although a large majority of women are never victims of rape and not all men are rapists, many women live in fear of the possibility. Due to the very existence of rape, women and girls change and limit their behaviour.

For you to visualise instances of day-to-day rape culture, below are some examples:

- Blaming the victim – saying something along the lines of "She was asking for it" or "She shouldn't have worn those sorts of clothes"

- Sexually explicit jokes – e.g. jokes about rape and jokes degrading and stereotyping women

- Trivialising and allowing sexual assault – saying something such as "Boys will be boys"

- Slut-shaming – stigmatising a female for seeming promiscuous or behaving in a way that is deemed to be sexually provocative

- Objectifying women – treating women like objects rather than living beings (the image of women being objects rather than humans makes the idea of sexual assault seem acceptable from the perspective of the person objectifying)

- Teaching girls to be submissive and overly polite as they grow up, including taking the blame for things as well as being excessively apologetic (this may at first seem like a very trivial issue – however, a 15-year-old girl who was molested by a boy from one of the top private schools in London said in her testimony that she did not struggle as she wanted to be "as polite as possible")

The examples above are some common instances by which rape culture can be identified. It may also be thought badly upon to teach women to avoid getting in tricky situations rather than teaching men not to rape. Nevertheless, regardless of how many times someone may be taught not to do something, the outcome may remain the same and they may still act inappropriately. For this reason, it is always important to still be able to protect yourself in a worst-case scenario.

A recent event that has once again sparked discussion about rape culture and safety on the streets is the case of Sarah Everard.

On 3 March 2021, Sarah Everard, a 33-year-old marketing executive, was walking home to Brixton Hill from one of her friend's houses near Clapham Common. She had been on the phone to her boyfriend for around 15 minutes and had told him that they would meet the next day. However, Sarah Everard neither met her boyfriend the next day nor reached home safely.

When her boyfriend was unable to contact her, he began to get extremely concerned and called the police to help locate her whereabouts. The police began an investigation and checked the security cameras near where she was walking on 3 March. Sarah was seen on the phone for around 15 minutes at 9.00pm. Later, at 9.28pm, with the use of a doorbell camera, she was seen walking past and four minutes later registered on the dashcam of a police car passing by. Investigators considered the possibility that the police officer used his police warrant card to convince Everard to get into the car.

On 9 March, the Kent Police arrested Wayne Couzens, a 48-year-old Metropolitan Police constable and firearms officer, on suspicion of kidnapping. At a hearing on 9 July, Couzens pleaded guilty to rape and murder. Not only is it horrific that rape and murder such as this happen at all, but even more so the fact that it was a police officer who committed this crime. This example really helps represent the flaws in society and provides further reasons for why one must always be prepared for the unexpected.

Recently, various movements have addressed rape culture in the 21st century, such as 'SlutWalk' and 'Me Too', both of which have helped victims of rape culture share their stories through social media and the use of hashtags. The most recent of these movements being 'Everyone's Invited'.

Like 'Me Too' and 'SlutWalk', 'Everyone's Invited' is a movement primarily based upon victims of sexual assault sharing their stories on social media to help lead to the global exposure and eventual eradication of rape culture. This was founded in June 2020 by Soma Sara, who herself had experienced rape culture. Since then, over 50,000 testimonies have been submitted with the hope that it allows many victims "a sense of relief, catharsis, empowerment" alongside "a feeling of community and hope". It is named 'Everyone's Invited' to show that anyone may give their testimonies anonymously to help spread awareness of the issue.

On the 'Everyone's Invited' website and on Instagram, horrific first-person testimonies can be read, some even written by girls as young as nine. In these accounts, young girls look back at traumatic events they suffered ranging from intimate photos of them being shared without consent to being intoxicated and assaulted at parties.

This truly helped me understand the harsh, unfathomable reality that, regardless of a person's extensive education, they may still commit sexual assault. For this reason, it could pay off knowing how to defend oneself from unexpected situations. In eight out of ten cases, people are sexually assaulted by someone they know.

So, is the probability really that high? Yes. The statistics I have given at the beginning of this chapter only considered those who had spoken about their experiences and reported them. However, thousands of victims choose not to speak up about such events due to blackmail, shame, politeness etc. Just from 'Everyone's Invited', thousands of people spoke up regarding their experiences for the first time, yet I am sure thousands remain who have decided not to talk about it. The true number of sexual assault cases may never be known.

THE GODDESS DURGA

In Hinduism, women have always played a significant role in life, and having grown up in an environment surrounded by successful and respected women, I find no dearth of examples of women who demonstrate strength and the ability to conquer their own fears.

When writing this book, I felt that the Hindu goddess Durga, a symbol of feminine power, destroyer of evil spirits and saviour of good, was the perfect representation of a woman.

The goddess Durga is a multidimensional goddess, with many names, personas and facets. In Hindu mythology, she is depicted riding a lion or a tiger in the 'Abhay Mudra' pose, signifying the assurance of freedom from fear. She is also shown to have multiple arms, holding different weapons, that can attack and protect from every direction.

An interesting tale around the goddess Durga is one of her fierce battles with the shape-shifting demon king

Mahishasura, who had been blessed in such a way that no man would be able to kill him. Empowered by the boon, Mahishasura began to terrorise the whole world. In a war with the gods, he defeated their army and had them running helter-skelter. The gods all approached the Trinity of Brahma, Vishnu and Shiva for help. Together, the Trinity and the gods combined their forces to call upon goddess Durga, the female form of the life-force energy of the universe. Goddess Durga then faced Mahishasura and routed him and his armies, restoring peace and order.

For me, Durga is like a one-person army embodying multiple special skills, making her the perfect match for evil. The symbolism of goddess Durga – the ability to defeat fear with ferocity and power and conquer darkness with light and energy through the combination of inner strength and an arsenal of tools – is extremely inspirational and in line with the theme of this book.

The techniques of Kung Fu, presented in this book, are like the tools every person should have, ready to defend from every direction.

KUNG FU

The number of issues regarding one's safety is simply immeasurable, and anyone may be at risk daily. Regardless of how many police officers are distributed throughout the city, however many criminals are arrested, crime will still exist. How can you defend yourself if ever caught in a situation of this kind? That is where Kung Fu comes in handy.

When most people think of Kung Fu, immediately thoughts such as 'Kung Fu Panda' rush to their minds. Others may think of it as simply a martial art, just like karate, boxing and others. In reality, Kung Fu is far from just being a martial art; it is a way of life.

In the Western world, Kung Fu is simply thought to be a martial art that originated in China. It may also be referred to less commonly as 'Wushu' or 'Quanfa'. However, in China, Kung Fu refers to any study, learning or practice that requires dedication, patience and time to complete. Its ancient, original meaning refers to any discipline or skill achieved through hard work and practice.

Chinese martial arts can be traced back to primitive society, where hunting and defence were required daily to survive. At first, this only comprised of basic skills, such as chopping, stabbing and cleaving, alongside the use of other weapons. China's Yellow Emperor, Huangdi, who took the throne in 2698 BC, began to formalise martial arts. Initially, he invented a form of wrestling aimed to teach troops, which involved the use of horned helmets. This was called 'Horn Butting' or 'Jiao Di'. Later, Jiao Di was improved upon to include joint locks, strikes and blocks (similar to the ones in modern Kung Fu) and became a sport during the Qin Dynasty (approximately 221 BC).

Buddhism also played a key role in the origin of Kung Fu. Buddhism came to China from India as relations between the two countries grew from 58–76 AD. Alongside this, the concept of Buddhism grew more popular in China as monks were sent back and forth between the countries, bringing foreign ideas and beliefs along with them. An Indian monk by the name of Bodhidharma is mentioned in the martial arts history books. Bodhidharma preached to monks at the newly formed Shaolin Temple in China and is believed to have changed not only their way of thinking by promoting concepts such as humility and restraint but also may have taught the monks martial arts movements.

Though this is disputed by some, once Bodhidharma arrived, these monks became famous martial arts practitioners that worked vigorously and daily at their craft.

Initially, Kung Fu was only an elite art practised by those with power, such as emperors and the rich. However, due to occupations by the Japanese, French and British, the Chinese began to encourage martial arts experts to open their doors and teach what they knew to the native masses with an aim for any citizen to be able to help expel foreign invaders.

Due to the rich and long history of Chinese martial arts, there are over 400 substyles of Kung Fu. Kung Fu is most known to be split into two larger sections: northern and southern.

The northern styles, such as Shaolin Kung Fu (named because the style originated in Shaolin temples), Long Fist, Eagle Claw and Monkey style tend to attach a reasonable level of importance to kicks and wide stances. The southern styles, such as Wing Chun, Hung Gar and Choy Li Fut, focus more on the utilisation of the hands and narrower stances.

The substyle of Kung Fu referred to in this book is Wing Chun, the world's most popular form of southern Kung Fu and the form which I have been studying for several years now.

Wing Chun is all about close-quarters combat on your feet. It tends to be used for the stage in a fight that comes before grappling. Wing Chun is designed to defend yourself on the street and in everyday life.

Wing Chun's history is shrouded in the past and is still a mystery. Documentation of the art began appearing during the era of Wing Chun master Leung Jan (1826–1901). However, legend has it that its origins come from Bruce Lee's Wing Chun teacher, Yip Man, popularised in the Western world by the *Ip Man* films.

One of the legends of how Wing Chun originated goes like this:

After the Qing government destroyed southern Shaolin styles and its temples, a Qing warlord offered to marry a woman named Yim Wing Chun, only to be faced with rejection. The warlord agreed to stop pursuing her if she could beat him in a martial arts match. Yim trained with a Buddhist nun named Ng Mui, who taught her a nameless style of fighting. Her training later helped her defeat the warlord, and she eventually married a man name Leung Bac-Chou. She taught her husband the style of fighting she had learned, and he gave it the name 'Wing Chun' after her.

Balance is important to all martial artists, and this is especially true for Wing Chun practitioners, who are trained to maintain a good defensive posture. In addition, Wing Chun practitioners keep their elbows close to the body and tend towards a high, narrow stance. Their arms are kept in front of the vital points of their centreline (an invisible line that spans the throat, nose, eyes, solar plexus and groin). All attacks begin from this stable, protective position. This may be contrasted with other martial arts, such as karate, which tends to use big kicks and long, circular motions (which may, in a street-fight situation, take too long and which require far more energy than rapid, effective movements).

Wing Chun practitioners are also known for their ability to overwhelm opponents with rapid strikes and kicks. They like to deliver simultaneous attacks, trap opponents and manipulate them into immobile positions.

So, is Kung Fu (more specifically Wing Chun) really effective? Some martial arts will always be more effective than others, and to answer the question of which one is the most effective for a street fight, we need to first understand the nature of these sorts of fights. They usually start from a distance but get closer as the attacker gets aggressive verbally and attempts to get close enough to both push and punch. It is much the same with a mugging. There may be no warning of an attack as there is in a robbery or a scene of sexual assault, but the attacker will get close enough to you to attack.

For a Wing Chun practitioner, this is exactly the kind of situation that they practise for, since Wing Chun is a close-combat form of martial arts. The use of rapid movements to vital body parts, in this scenario, will be extremely effective in ending a fight within seconds, allowing the practitioner to leave the area without the risk of being followed again.

As Hélio Gracie, the godfather of Brazilian Jiu-Jitsu, used to say, "Always assume that your opponent is going to be bigger, stronger and faster than you, so that you learn to rely on technique, timing and leverage rather than brute strength." In the context of learning to defend yourself, this forms the very basis of the Kung Fu techniques I have outlined later in the book – techniques that help nullify advantages your attacker may have in size, strength or speed.

THE BENEFITS OF KUNG FU

For sincere practitioners of Kung Fu, it becomes much more than a martial art; it becomes a way of life. That may appear to be hyperbolic, but I do believe that Kung Fu can change one's life completely – both physically and mentally.

Physical health

Kung Fu helps a practitioner develop not only strength but also flexibility. This is contrasted to many other workouts which focus on either strength or flexibility. If you want to get physically fit without having to just do a simple collection of drills and static exercises which you may get bored of extremely soon, Kung Fu is ideal. The practice of kicks, punches and pivots of the hips helps stretch the entire body and develop flexibility alongside increasing strength. Not only does one get to learn new techniques, one can also stay fit at the same time.

During Kung Fu training, drills can really help work up one's heart rate, thus helping build cardiovascular endurance. Increasing cardiovascular endurance improves a person's oxygen uptake in the lungs and heart, which helps them sustain physical activity for longer. When in a fight, having the ability to sustain for longer than your opponent is vital and further enhances your probability of gaining the upper hand.

Kung Fu practitioners also tend to increase their muscle mass during training, which helps their body become more toned overall. Both punching and kicking repetitively require a lot of strength and demand that the muscles in your arms, legs and core work extremely hard. Furthermore, muscle mass and metabolism are connected. The more muscle mass one has, the higher the metabolic demand becomes. This means a person would burn more calories, even while their body is at rest. This also contributes to weight loss on a larger scale. Having gained more muscle mass, now that more calories are burned daily, it is only expected that weight will be lost.

A key benefit of practising Kung Fu is the improvement of one's reflexes and building muscle memory. Fast reflexes are essential to becoming a good martial artist. Whether it is sparring or a street fight, being able to block and dodge your opponent's attacks in time is crucial to every martial artist. Through repetition and practice, your reflexes will improve and you will notice evidently faster reaction times throughout your daily life.

I've seen this borne out in my own experience. I regularly play squash. When playing squash, your reactions to your opponent's shots and movements need to be as quick as possible. Within just a few months of Kung Fu training, I began to see a noticeable improvement in my ability to react to my opponent's shots, moving towards the ball faster to gain an advantageous position.

As well as this, Kung fu requires mobility and agility when sparring. Practising Kung Fu is a fabulous way to improve your body's ability to move faster and as efficiently as possible in a fight. Over time, it is guaranteed that you will notice greater speed, especially if you practise a lot of footwork.

Kung Fu requires its practitioners to have a high degree of stability and coordination. When it comes to executing moves and blocking attacks, one needs awareness and stability to succeed. With practice, both qualities start improving, particularly during sparring, and you will seldom find yourself in an unstable, vulnerable position during a fight as your body starts learning newer habits of reaction.

Other health benefits may include lowering blood pressure and increasing blood circulation, strengthening your immune system and improving sleep quality. Especially during training, repetitive movement can act like high-intensity interval training. This helps slow down your resting heart rate and lowers blood pressure.

Of course, the key benefit of Kung Fu is the ability to defend oneself. If you are ever caught in a situation where you have no choice but to fight to prevent yourself from being harmed, Kung Fu will always give you leverage.

Mental health

Numerous studies have shown that Kung Fu can help improve mental health as well.

Kung Fu helps a person to release stress. Kung Fu teaches practitioners to draw energy in, focusing on good breathing techniques and visualisation. These techniques can be used in training but are also helpful in everyday situations, such as when bombarded with work, when in arguments or even in a fight. Intense physical activity itself is always effective at purging stress.

Practising Kung Fu is also a fantastic way to build solid confidence and self-esteem. Simply knowing that you can defend yourself in any situation builds confidence within oneself. I, for example, began to feel more confident in public spaces or late at night having started to practise Kung Fu. One of my instructors who as a child was below average height once told me about his experiences of being bullied at school as well as always crossing the road to stay away from a few people in his school – before he learned Kung Fu. Interestingly, as he began to practise on a regular basis, his increase in confidence translated to how he physically carried himself. And he started realising that now the bullies automatically give him a wide berth.

Furthermore, students of Kung Fu may also appreciate a sense of affirmation when learning a new technique or achieving a new grade. Another immense confidence booster comes when a practitioner sees clear improvements in their fighting skills (sparring), coordination and physique.

All martial arts place a heavy emphasis on discipline. Kung Fu in particular focuses on the idea that patience and insight win out over rash, violent and aggressive behaviour. This discipline tends to be taught right from the start, and practitioners develop more self-discipline due to their training. It's taught that to achieve goals, one needs to be calm and practise self-control. Understanding that patience and hard work pay off not only helps a person within Kung Fu training but is also something they take with them and incorporate into their daily lives.

Improving concentration comes naturally with Kung Fu practice. A wandering mind gives space for poor techniques. There are many forms of Kung Fu that include forms of meditation that help focus the mind and release any and all distractions.

I strongly believe that to overcome hardships in life, one needs to strengthen one's willpower and ability to persevere. By training in Kung Fu, one gains an understanding that taking an alternate path when a difficulty arises is a viable option but turning back gets you nowhere.

As a Kung Fu practitioner myself, I have personally experienced most of the benefits mentioned, and ever since I began training in Kung Fu, I have benefited in a variety of ways that, I feel, now make my daily life easier and more balanced.

WHY NOT USE SOMETHING ELSE?

When on the street or indoors, there are hundreds of options on how to defend yourself against a possible threat. However, some will forever remain more effective and reliable than others. Before I begin introducing you to Kung Fu techniques with which you can defend yourself, I will first give other common methods used by many and weigh out whether they are truly beneficial or not.

However, before we get to even discussing what to do in a theoretical situation in which you are being assaulted or attacked, we must first discuss how to avoid situations such as these in the first place. Regardless of whether you are an experienced Kung Fu practitioner or have only read this book, it is always advised to avoid situations such as these and avoid having to fight. It's mostly best to just run and distance yourself from the aggressor. Of course, you would be the best judge of the situation you may end up in.

For example, if you were at a party and someone began to assault you in any form, and you are already in close proximity to them, you could use Kung Fu to your advantage to prevent them from further endangering you. In contrast to this, if you are alone on the street and a couple of people are following you, it would be best to run due to the lower probability of succeeding in fighting two people at once. Furthermore, you would never know what other weapons they may be carrying with them which could fatally injure you. However, of course, there will always be instances where one isn't able to escape from the location.

There is a high probability that you may have heard these basic recommendations when walking alone, yet it is always important to be reminded of them. Firstly, always be prepared. Before stepping out onto the streets, you should know where you are going and how you plan on getting there. You should also try to carry a mobile phone and some cash. A mobile phone can be used for calling for help, and cash may be useful to prevent someone from attacking you by paying them off. When walking on the streets, I am aware that everyone has a different personality and may have a variety of insecurities which they may try to hide from others; however, you must always attempt to look confident and assertive to help yourself seem less vulnerable and more in control.

When walking, it is often very tempting to pull out your earphones and listen to some music or maybe check your messages and keep up-to-date with what's going on in your social life. There are two main senses which play a vital role when walking, one of them being sight, and the other being sound. However, the visual field of the human eye spans around a 120-degree arc. Even so, most of this is one's peripheral vision. If distracted by a screen, then that immediately prevents you from seeing any possible threats approaching from that span of 120 degrees around you. However, there are still another 240 degrees around you which the human eye can't cover. For this reason, it is vital to check behind you every few minutes whilst walking. However, when you are not turned around, sound is the only sense which you can rely upon. You guessed it, if you have earphones in while walking then you also cut off the other 240 degrees from your consciousness and would not be able to tell if someone is approaching you from behind.

Not only should you keep away phones and headsets, but other valuables should not be noticeable, such as expensive rings or necklaces. Finally, you should try to 'go against the flow'. By this, I mean that you should try to walk in such a manner that you are facing oncoming traffic as this makes it extremely difficult for people to cycle or drive up behind you and steal from you or attack you. If this means crossing the road on your way to a destination, it's something I would recommend.

If you do ever feel unsafe whilst walking down a street, it is always recommended that you go into a shop and let someone know about your situation so that they too may help keep you safe. From here, you would be able to call someone for help knowing you are in a secure location.

Many girls rely on handheld weapons to protect themselves during their daily lives just in case someone tries to sexually assault them or rob them. One of the most common items that may be found is the pepper spray. A pepper spray is easily portable and can be concealed and carried in a handbag without much hassle. It generally tends to be non-lethal and does not have any long-lasting effects on the person it is used upon. It provides the opportunity to end an attack without the use of physical force or extreme violent action. Pepper spray is relatively easy to use and does not require any intensive training to effectively use it.

However, a pepper spray is at best a partial solution. It often does not work on everyone. This can be due to mental illness or intoxicated states of mind due to the use of drugs, which prevent them from being affected. Many people can also just fight through the effects of pepper spray and continue their attack. It also runs a huge risk of over-contamination. When in a stressful situation, people who are not trained usually tend to empty an entire canister of pepper spray when they use it rather than the ideal small, controlled, targeted burst. This means that anyone in proximity may suffer the effects. Worse still, it may even incapacitate the person deploying it.

Most importantly, it may be difficult to deploy in stressful and violent situations. The target area is minuscule (the eyes), and the person being aimed at may be wearing glasses or a mask, which could negate the intended effects of pepper spray. Often, by the time you notice the attack commencing, it would already be too late to search through your bag or pockets to pull out your pepper spray, uncap it and use it. This would take at least ten seconds, and by that time it would be too late.

Deploying pepper spray also has various legal ramifications. In the United Kingdom, it is "unlawful for a member of the public to have it." The law states that it is prohibited as a "weapon of whatever description designed or adapted for the discharge of any noxious liquid, gas or other thing." The possession of pepper spray is a criminal offence that is punishable by up to ten years in prison. I honestly doubt whether it's worth the risk.

Another weapon that some may think of is a pocket knife. However, a knife only tends to be useful in being a deterrent. If an attacker were to see you brandishing a knife, they would question their choice in harassing you and may back off. However, if they don't back off, for the knife to be used effectively, the user must be very skilful and have been trained to use a knife for self-defence. Frankly, knives are quite useless if you don't know how to use them. Even worse, a knife can be turned against you and used against you if you were to drop it or if it were knocked out of your hand.

Let's say you were in a self-defence situation; if you manage to stab or slash someone, regardless of what they did to you, you are most probably going to go to jail. This is since stabbing or slashing is likely to cause permanent damage, a lifelong disability or death. No matter how justified you may be in defending yourself, if you do end up killing someone, you will be confronted with serious consequences. In most jurisdictions, (counter)attacking someone with a knife is considered assault with a deadly weapon. Even without harming anyone, it remains illegal to carry a knife in public.

Another common item carried by women is a personal alarm. These alarms have buttons that, when pressed, sound off a loud siren that does not stop until you stop it. They may also alert a response centre or a family member when help is needed. However, personal alarms only give a false sense of security to the user and don't really have any guarantee of protecting them from anything. They may be useful if others around you can immediately help; for example, at a party, if someone were to begin sexually or violently assaulting you, equipping a personal alarm may bring attention to yourself, and someone may turn to help you. But will someone always be there to help? Consider this: it's 3.00am and you are awoken by the sound of an alarm in the distance, most likely a car alarm elsewhere in the neighbourhood. You're still half asleep and just want to sleep. What would you do? What would most people do? Most people would simply roll over and hope it turns off soon so that they can go back to sleep.

Alarms have become so common in one's daily life that most people don't pay attention to them unless it's a genuine nuisance to them. The alarms themselves operate on the idea that a criminal doesn't want to be seen committing a crime. There have to be people around to hear it and curious enough to see where the alarm is coming from. Furthermore, the criminal needs to care about the consequences of being caught. Many criminals may be intoxicated and unbothered by consequences, whereas others plan to follow through with their plan and leave quickly having completed it. The alarms have to be loud too, otherwise they may get drowned out by the sound of traffic or not be heard by those indoors over other noises. Even though personal alarms are fully legal and easy to access, before considering equipping one, you must fully consider their effectiveness.

No object is 100% effective when dealing with the ultimate unpredictable variable: humans.

I'm sure by now you must be wondering,

"What really works then?"

"Is there anything both effective and reliable?"

In the sentence, "No object is 100% effective when dealing with the ultimate unpredictable variable: humans", the keyword is 'object'.

The most reliable defence mechanism one can use is oneself. This is because a person can truly only rely on themselves and have faith in their ability. If certain abilities and reflexes are ingrained into a person, they would be able to rely on this more than something such as a personal alarm, which has no guarantee of safety.

Being able to master certain techniques builds a sense of confidence within oneself of knowing that you would be capable of preventing any sort of assault.

Let's therefore step into the specific forms and techniques of Wing Chun Kung Fu.

FORMS IN KUNG FU

Let's now step into the core principles on which Kung Fu is based. In line with most Chinese martial arts, 'forms' are an essential part of Wing Chun Kung Fu training.

A form is a combination of different stances, footwork patterns, blocking movements, evasive actions and striking and kicking techniques. They are created to represent the fundamental moves used in a real fighting experience, all combined into one.

Different martial arts styles have unique characteristics which can be clearly distinguished in the execution and movements of the forms that represent them. Thus, northern styles can be distinguished and differentiated from their southern counterparts (including Wing Chun).

Training one's forms serves multiple purposes. Forms teach practitioners to train the body to move in countless different patterns, such as advancing, retreating, defending and countering in time. With sufficient practice, the movements included in forms become reflexive actions that can be used by a practitioner spontaneously in an encounter.

Wing Chun Kung Fu comprises three open-handed forms, one wooden dummy form and two weapon forms. For the purpose of this book, I'll focus on the first of the open-handed forms, the Si Nim Tau, which provides the key to the techniques one needs to know to defend themselves from most likely attacks. I will still talk a bit about the wooden dummy form and weapon forms, though I will not refer to them much after.

Si Nim Tau

The first, and most important, form learned and practised in Wing Chun is called Si Nim Tau, literally translated as 'a little idea'. The meditative nature of Si Nim Tau makes thoughts of daily matters of love, hate, money, work etc. disappear.

Si Nim Tau comprises the foundations of Kung Fu upon which all succeeding forms and techniques depend. When practising this, fundamental rules of balance and body structure are developed. In fact, Ip Ching, one of the five grandmasters of Yip Man, said, "Si Nim Tau is not just the beginning course but an important foundation. When we learn English, we first learn the 26 letters of the alphabet. If we cannot handle the pronunciation of each letter, then our English will never be good. The magnitude of the first form, Si Nim Tau, in Wing Chun is the same as that of letters in English."

Si Nim Tau comprises eight parts, and each part is a range of techniques and changes in the practitioner's energy. In five out of the eight parts, the left hand leads the movement followed by the right hand. In the other three parts, both hands are used simultaneously. Si Nim Tau does not consist of any footwork, and this is only later introduced in the next form.

Si Nim Tau starts from an initial stance called Gee Kim Yeung Ma, which focuses on building leg muscles and balance from standing and connecting the whole body's energy to the ground. One's legs are slightly bent with toes facing inwards and the body centred, and their hands are placed by their sides in a 90-degree angle with the fist facing forward.

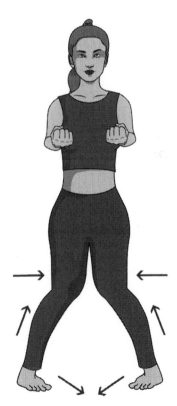

Below I have included a simplified version of the eight parts of Si Nim Tau, which I will refer to later.

Section 1: 4 movements

1. Cross hands down
2. Cross hands up
3. Separate hands
4. Bring them back

Section 2: 6 movements

1. Left punch
2. Circling hand
3. Bring hand back

Repeat on the right

Section 3: 40 movements

1. Left palm up, hand out
2. Hand rotates and moves across the body
3. Guard hand back
4. Bridge hand
5. Bridge hand outwards
6. Hand rotates and moves across the body
7. Guarding hand back

Repeat the last 4 movements 2 more times

8. Palm strike to the shoulder line
9. Centre the hand
10. Centre palm strike
11. Circling hand
12. Bring hand back

Repeat all movements on the right

Section 4: 13 movements

1. Downwards left pressing hand
2. Downwards right pressing hand
3. Double press behind
4. Double press in front
5. Double bar hand in front of the chest
6. Double chop to either side
7. Double bar hand in front of the chest
8. Double sinking hands
9. Double lifting hand
10. Double poking hand
11. Double pressing hand
12. Double raising hand
13. Double hand back

Section 5: 10 movements

1. Left outward slap
2. Left palm up hand

3. Palm up neck hit
4. Circling hand
5. Bring hand back

Repeat on the right

Section 6: 16 movements

1. Left palm out
2. Sink the hand
3. Sweeping hand
4. Palm up hand
5. Circling hand
6. Low palm strike
7. Circling hand
8. Bring hand back

Repeat on the right

Section 7: 10 movements

1. Left wing hand
2. Left palm up hand
3. Left low palm strike
4. Left circling hand
5. Bring hand back

Repeat on the right

Section 8: 13 movements

1. Left hand down
2. Replace with right in twisting motion
3. Right hand down
4. Replace with the left in twisting motion
5. Left hand down
6. Replace with right in twisting motion
7. Right hand down
8. Left punch
9. Right punch
10. Left punch (stays forward)
11. Right punch (both hands now ahead)
12. Twisting grip hands
13. Bring hands back

Si Nim Tau is a vital part of Wing Chun which every practitioner must master before progressing to more advanced levels.

Chum Kiu

The second open-handed form of Wing Chun Kung Fu is Chum Kiu, literally meaning 'sinking bridge'. Chum Kiu primarily focuses on coordinated movement of the practitioner's body mass and entry techniques to "bridge the gap between them and their opponent", alongside moving in such a way that it disrupts their opponent's structure and balance, thus giving the practitioner the upper hand.

Within Chum Kiu, close-range techniques utilising the elbows and knees are developed. It also teaches methods of recovering one's position and centrelines when in a position where one's structure has been lost.

Biu Jee

The third open-handed form of Wing Chun Kung Fu is called Biu Jee, translated as 'thrusting fingers'. This is composed of both extreme short- and long-range techniques and low kicks/sweeps, alongside things which may be "emergency, last-resource techniques" to counterattack when the practitioner's structure and centreline have been compromised in a situation, such as where they have been seriously injured.

Alongside pivots and steps developed in Chum Kiu, another degree of freedom is implemented involving more upper-body movements and stretching, which results in more power. This includes movements such as elbow strikes and finger thrusts to the throat (to end a fight as soon as possible).

A common Wing Chun saying is "Biu Jee doesn't go out the door." This means that one should never use Biu Jee unless it's required in a worst-case scenario, as it could be fatal for your opponent. Even if you are required to defend yourself on the street, you still shouldn't bypass the law and go to the point where your attacker is helpless and you continue to attack them – while attack is inbuilt into Wing Chun forms, the core purpose remains to defend.

Muk Yan Jong

Muk Yan Jong, translated as 'wooden man post', is Wing Chun Kung Fu's most advanced form and comprises 116 movements across eight sections. It uses a wooden dummy to help advanced students practise and perfect their techniques. The arms of the Wing Chun wooden dummy can represent attacks that have to be blocked or obstacles for the student to overcome in order to attack the trunk of the dummy. The leg of the dummy has to be manoeuvred around and attacked by the student during the form and helps with balance and correct positioning.

Luk Dim Boon Kwun

The first weapon form of Wing Chun Kung Fu is the Luk Dim Boon Kwun, translated as 'six-and-a-half-point pole'. This form is taught using a long eight-foot pole and uses the shoulder as the centreline. It uses the long-bridge technique in both arms to concentrate power into the endpoint of the pole. The form has six different techniques, which are repeated through application in different directions along with the half technique of dropping the pole.

Baat Cham Do

The second weapon form of Wing Chun Kung Fu is the Baat Cham Do, translated as 'eight cutting knives'. This form, taught using a pair of Wing Chun Dao or 'butterfly knives', reinforces the underlying Wing Chun principles seen in the other hand forms, for instance, economy of motion, deflection and advanced footwork. It develops additional power and strength in the stance. Furthermore, due to the weight of the Baat Cham Dao and the use of a deep stance, this form greatly improves wrist, arm and leg strength if trained regularly and correctly.

PUNCHES IN KUNG FU

"Attack is the best form of defence." This phrase captures an important characteristic of a lot of the Kung Fu techniques I will describe.

The techniques described in the next chapter are primarily defence techniques. If you only use these techniques, you will prevent the singular attack at that moment, but the first attack will most likely be followed by more attacks after. Let's consider this from the perspective of an assaulter. They may throw a punch towards you expecting it to make contact; however, you suddenly block their attack. They're shocked for a few seconds, trying to process what just happened. However, now they realise that you know how to defend yourself and throw more punches with a greater variety. This would be an issue. The fight should finish as soon as possible, but simply defending and letting them attack won't finish the fight. Therefore, those few seconds you gain whilst the attacker is shocked are when you attack in such a manner that they don't attempt to assault you again.

The counterattacks you can use are countless, but I'll introduce you to the most simple and effective one: the punches.

There are various types of punches one can deliver. Furthermore, each of these punches can be delivered to different parts of your opponent's body. Each of these is more effective than others in different situations and based on several uncontrolled variables, such as height and size.

Firstly, let's discuss where it is most recommended to land punches. A simple way to think about this is to consider where all the vital organs in the body are which aren't protected by bone. A lot of the vital attack points in the human body are aligned with the centreline of the body, which most Kung Fu stances try to protect. Note that I refer to punches in the plural. Always assume that one punch is not going to be enough, and follow through with more in a continuous movement.

Punches to the nose

The nose is an excellent spot to punch someone if you don't necessarily need to knock them out. Scientifically speaking, a light punch to the nose is also formidable. This is as it only takes relatively small force to break a person's nose, anywhere from 30–40 newtons when hitting sideways or upwards. On an approximate basis, most inexperienced people can easily deliver a force of around 500 newtons in a punch.

A punch to the nose is unfathomably disorienting, thanks to the excruciating pain of the broken nose cartilage and all the blood that goes with it. The nose is also connected to your eyes by tear ducts, meaning damage to the nose often results in tears, leading to a temporary loss of vision – one of the best advantages to have during a one-on-one confrontation.

Punches to the neck

The human neck is an exceptionally vulnerable spot. For the side of the neck, a sharp strike downward will hit the vagus nerve. The vagus nerve is the longer cranial nerve that is responsible for carrying a lot of information from the brain to the rest of your body. A sharp strike to the vagus nerve can result in dizziness, disorientation or even unconsciousness. Also, one's trachea and larynx are found in the throat. The larynx is what allows air to pass through to the lungs through the trachea. If someone's larynx or trachea were punched, they would not be able to breathe for a few seconds and could even pass out from lack of oxygen and the inability to respire.

Punches to the liver

The liver is located on the upper-right portion of your abdomen, just below the ribs.

A liver shot is an incredibly painful experience. A punch shocks the liver, the largest glandular organ in the human body and one of the body's centres of blood circulation, and causes the victim to lose focus and drive, as well as causing a feeling of breathlessness in the victim.

Punches to the solar plexus

The solar plexus is located right under the chest and just above the stomach.

Hitting the solar plexus is extremely effective. The reason is that there are a lot of nerves located at the solar plexus and your diaphragm (which helps you breathe) is located right behind it. When the solar plexus is hit, the diaphragm begins to spasm and the person affected becomes unable to breathe alongside being greeted with a lot of pain.

Punches to the groin

A punch to the groin is tremendously agonising, regardless of who your opponent is. Remember when I mentioned the vagus nerve earlier? Well, it is an extremely long and sensitive nerve that runs from your face to your groin. As the vagus nerve is so long and sensitive, it is one of the pathways along which pain is sent when someone is kicked in the crotch. This is the reason being hurt in the groin sends pain throughout one's body.

I would not recommend attempting this counterattack over other attacks. The reason is that the chance of hitting the groin is not always guaranteed. Many people wear baggy clothing, which can prevent your hand from reaching the intended target area and reduce the power in the punch. Furthermore, it may seem unnatural to have to punch at such a low angle. Even kicks to the groin may not be as effective because legs may also get caught by jeans or other clothing.

I would highly recommend avoiding areas such as the forehead and the upper chest, as they are both protected by dense bone and may end up damaging your hand too (which is a lose-lose). You can choose which area of the body to strike depending on how tall your opponent is relative to yourself and what will be the quickest.

The Wing Chun punch

Now let me tell you about one of the most vital methods of punching: the straight punch, also known as the 'Wing Chun punch'.

Learning this punch is initially confusing for many martial artists because it feels unnatural. Most people consider the natural human punch to be a very wide-swinging punch where one must swing their arms in wide arcs to pummel the opponent. This punch is in fact not very effective and is also often easily deflected.

The Wing Chun punch uses a vertical fist. A vertical fist means that the knuckles are aligned vertically with the body (parallel, as if you're holding a bottle in front of you upwards), whereas most other punches from boxing or martial arts are horizontal to the body (perpendicular). Having a vertical fist helps keep the punch straight.

Before providing tips on how to improve this straight punch and make it more powerful, let's discuss some of the benefits.

"The best defence is to be invisible. If you cannot be, learn Wing Chun" (Sigong Wong Shun Leung – one of Yip Man's former students).

The near invisibility of this punch is achieved by several factors which all work together:

- Simple geometry helps keeps the straight punch near to invisible. The shortest distance between two points is a straight line. This 'shortest distance' therefore allows the fastest travel, which is used in a Wing Chun punch. It starts in front of you, at the centre, and follows a straight and short path to the target. In Wing Chun, this straight path is called the 'centre line'.

- The punch requires you to stand close to your opponent. Being close also gives your opponent less time to see your strike coming.

- One must not 'pull back' to throw the Wing Chun punch. 'Pulling back' telegraphs the fact that you are about to throw a punch.

Another key part of the Wing Chun punch is its accuracy. The punch's straight path allows it to be exactly accurate. Accuracy means that less force is needed to get the desired effect because the straight path focuses the force directly onto the target and point of impact.

Here are some key points on executing the Wing Chun punch. You must keep your hands at or within your shoulder width and between chest and shoulder height.

Your elbows should be pointed down rather than out to the side. This protects your torso, whereas having your elbows outwards leaves a large target open to your opponent.

When practising the Wing Chun punch, it helps to think of it as a chain motion, such as a bicycle chain. Each punch goes over the other one which is retreating backwards. It is as if one fist is replacing the other each time.

A common mistake is striking downwards when punching. What happens is that you start to swing the fist down during the punching motion (sometimes it is so slight you do not notice it). If you hit a punching bag with a bare knuckle and you notice that you are chafing the skin on your knuckles, especially to the point of bleeding, you are most likely striking downward (and scraping your fist instead of striking into and through your target).

If this is happening to you, think of your punch like an arrow driving into your target. Not a hammer swinging down.

Once you train this finer detail, you will be presented with even more power behind your strike, as swinging down wastes energy. Hitting straight through your opponent concentrates the force onto the small area of the target.

If you just practise the correct punching motion repetitively for a minute daily, it will help build up your endurance alongside helping solidify your technique.

8 SELF-DEFENCE TECHNIQUES

This section aims to introduce you to basic yet highly effective Wing Chun techniques for eight different yet likely situations you may find yourself in. I do not doubt that you will be able to wrap your mind around these techniques and be able to apply them in a real-world situation.

An often-quoted line attributed to Bruce Lee is, "I fear not the man who has practised 10,000 kicks once, but I fear the man who has practised one kick 10,000 times."

If you practise these few techniques with a friend or family member and conceptualise how they work, they will soon become part of your reflexes and you will be able to have full faith in your capabilities of defending yourself.

1. Defending against the wrist grab

Grabbing the wrist is often the first step of an attack. The attacker is subconsciously aiming to take away your ability to hit back. It could be used to pull you closer or to prevent you from resisting (e.g. flailing or punching).

In this case, I'll teach you one move to help prevent this person from grabbing you in the first place (if your reaction time is fast enough) and two techniques to release yourself from the grip.

As the person reaches out and attempts to grab your wrist, you would perform the first two movements in Section 8 of Si Nim Tau.

Imagine the person is trying to grab your left wrist. You should straighten the left arm that is being grabbed and place your right hand facing upwards on your left elbow. It should look something like this:

From here, just as the person is about to grab your arm, you would pull your left hand back towards your body whilst twisting it and push down your right hand from your elbow to where your left hand had previously been. The position of your hands should look like this by the end of this movement:

The purpose of this is so that not only do you move your hand away from them, but you also hit their arm (just above the wrist) away in one smooth motion. This should be done before your wrist is grabbed, otherwise it will not have any effect. Furthermore, making impact with your hand on their arm would leave them in pain for a little bit of time, providing you with an opportunity to follow up with an attack, such as the punches we previously discussed.

If, however, you are not able to do this first technique in time, and the person does grab your wrist, there is a surprisingly simple technique you can use to get your hand out of their grip.

This technique is used at the end of most sections in Si Nim Tau. It is most evident at the end of Section 2, and I referred to it as 'circling hand'.

For the sake of understanding the images which I will refer to, they have their hands out at a 90-degree angle from the body, but this can be performed from any angle. This is because all this technique requires is the movement of the wrist, rather than the movement of the whole arm or elbow.

Start this method like this:

From here, you would move your fingers so that they are pointing towards you, without moving your wrist. From here, you would rotate your wrist 180 degrees:

This is a manoeuvre that does not actually require much strength. The reason the attacker's grip would falter from here is that it would not be possible for them to turn their hand 180 degrees without getting hurt, and so it would lead them to let go. You can take this brief opportunity to follow up with an attack.

The final technique I will introduce you to for wrist grabs is one used when the attacker pins both your hands against you with one hand (they would tend to do this with one hand so that they still have access to their other hand and do not fully immobilise themselves) or grabs you by your elbows. This method is the first section of Si Nim Tau. You would attempt to move your hands from the first position to the second position:

If you look carefully, you can see that the first image has the palms facing downwards, whereas the palms in the second image are facing the body. This is vital to understand. You will also notice that the person's left hand (our right) is on top of her right hand in the first image, but in the second image, it is closer to her. This is also important as if someone were to be grabbing your hands, their hand would be placed on your outer hand. If your outer hand was to move on the inside, then your opponent would no longer have control of your arms. To get from the first to the second position, all you must do is twist your forearm and wrist. When doing this, it is also important to push outwards away from your body to give yourself more room and move your opponent backwards.

Try this technique a few times and note the positions of your hands and how they switch positions when you do this.

2. Defending against a slap or swinging punch to the head

The swinging motion of the arm is the most common attack from inexperienced fighters on the street. This is as most people do not understand the concept I previously explained and how a straight punch is the most shocking and hardest to predict and therefore more effective.

In this instance, the person pulls their arm back in preparation to swing towards your head for either a slap or a punch. The move used to prevent this is called 'Fook

Sau', meaning 'bridging arm', one of the most useful moves in Wing Chun Kung Fu. I referenced this move earlier in Section 3 of Si Nim Tau as 'bridge hand'. This is because the arm is positioned in the shape of a bridge in this move.

Fook Sau is ideally used as a block or cover in Wing Chun when attacks are coming either to the head or slightly lower than head height. The inside of your wrist is used to guide the punch past the body. The hand is folded over the top to control the attacking hand and stop it from being pushed higher to hit your face. It is very important to keep the elbow in, just like at the start of Si Nim Tau. With the elbow kept at the right position, you will have no problem deflecting these sorts of strikes.

The hand is thrown forward in front of your shoulder to hit the opponent's arm with your forearm. Ideally, you are aiming to block at their bicep or upper arm, as this guarantees fully stopping their arm. If you make an impact on their forearm with your forearm, it may come down to strength, and if they are stronger, they could keep pushing forward and still hit your face.

The starting position for this movement would look like this:

The move would finish with the arm looking nearly the same but simply just further forward. Since this does hit the bicep of your opponent, they will receive a sudden shock and a wave of pain, alongside possible bruises to their upper arm.

Practise this technique with a friendly opponent a few times to make sure you begin to train your arms to react in the right way.

3. Defending against a straight punch to the face

The straight punch is another quite common punch used by those on the streets. This punch would tend to be directed straight at your face and may be used by an attacker closer to you to strike you on your nose or jaw. It is like the Wing Chun punch we discussed earlier.

The move to defend against a straight punch or a grab towards your face is called 'Pak Sau', meaning 'clapping hand'. Pak Sau, like Fook Sau, is part of the third section of Si Nim Tau, and I referenced it as 'palm strike to the shoulder line' in the Si Nim Tau section.

In Wing Chun, Pak Sau is a blocking technique that may be compared to a parry used in boxing. With Pak Sau, the hand comes directly out of the centre of the body to slap away an attacker's strike to one's head. Effective application of Pak Sau involves creating an angle of deflection through which the opponent's blow can be slapped away with minimal effort.

The Pak Sau is performed with the palm of your hand and should be used when your hand is on the outside of their arm. If you are on the outside of their arm when you use the Pak Sau, it will push their arm back into themselves and trap them. The hand movement would be across your body and look something like this:

If the Pak Sau is performed lower down the arm, towards the wrist for example, the attacker could easily counter by bending their arm and attacking instead with their elbow. It is important therefore to ensure you try to block further up the opponent's forearm (towards their elbow). This ensures you gain more control of the attacking arm and the opponent's body.

Practise this technique with a friendly opponent a few times to make sure you begin to train your arms to react in the right way and can correctly aim towards the upper arm rather than the lower arm.

4. Defending when grabbed by the shoulders from in front

This attack is usually used by stronger people with the aim to both intimidate and trap. In this attack, the person reaches forward and pushes your shoulders into a wall behind you with both their hands. They have decreased the distance between you, and the wall begins to dig into your spine. Your natural reaction may often be to panic and freeze.

The defence technique here is one of my favourite techniques because it is deceptively simple to execute and extremely effective. It is called 'Tok Sau', meaning 'lifting hands', and you move your hand in a lifting motion to remove the opponent's hands from your shoulder.

Most people would attempt to simply just grab their attacker's arms and attempt to push them away. However, doing this automatically pits you into a match of strength, and remember that our key should always be to prepare for an attacker who is physically stronger than us. Pushing a stronger attacker's arms away will always be extremely difficult. For this reason, it is best to stick to something which does not require any strength and is even more effective.

To execute Tok Sau, position your hands under their elbows like this:

From here you should push upwards and forwards towards them. This will lock their arms as you are pushing from the elbow and thus force them to move backwards and release their hands from your shoulders. It is necessary to make sure that your fingers point towards your opponent to ensure their elbows get locked, otherwise they will be given space to bend their elbows.

Practise this technique with a friendly opponent, ideally someone a lot stronger and bigger than you, a few times to understand how easy and effective this move is.

5. Defending from a punch to the stomach

The stomach region presents an attacker with a lower probability of missing. A punch to the stomach also knocks a person's wind out, shocking them temporarily, causing them to automatically drop their hands. Missing a stomach punch and hitting a person's abdomen has an even more powerful impact. It is important therefore to prevent an attacker's hand from reaching your stomach.

In this scenario, you would use a 'Gaun Sau', meaning 'sweeping hand', which is a sweeping motion with your hand across the body to protect your lower body. I refer to Gaun Sau as the sweeping hand in Section 6 of Si Nim Tau.

Gaun Sau is ideally used as a block or cover in Wing Chun Kung Fu when an attack is coming low, especially attacks to the ribs. This includes uppercuts and low hook punches. This is another one of the most essential blocks of the system as it is one of the few techniques that is used to protect the ribs. The area of the arm used by the practitioner is the outside of the forearm below the wrist.

The movement would look like this:

Your hand would not necessarily need to start from a high position as shown in the image above but should simply be able to quickly transfer into the movements required for Gaun Sau.

Practise this technique with a friendly opponent a few times to make sure you begin to train your arms to react in the right way.

6. Defending when being pulled by the hair from behind

Often the attack may happen when the attacker is quite close and you are in an environment where you are not expecting to be attacked. An example would be when you are at a party or in a club. In these circumstances, you are unable to predict the attack and need to prepare for responding immediately after being attacked. The next few techniques focus on these scenarios.

When someone grabs your hair and tugs you towards them, pain will shoot through your body alongside the shock and disbelief that this may be happening in an unexpected environment. The attacker may also be trying to pull you away from the crowd to a quieter place.

Normally, someone may try to resist this person pulling their hair and just use force to pull back and loosen their grip. I'll repeat that our purpose has to remain to assume that the attacker is stronger and we will likely not win in a strength battle. So, what should you do? Well, it is actually quite simple: you step backwards and move with the pull.

What? Just move with it? But how will that prevent their next attack?

Well, there are a few different reasons for this counterintuitive move.

Firstly, to stop the pain by yielding to the force of the pull.

Secondly, if you do stand still or try to resist them pulling your hair if they are stronger than you, there is a high chance you could lose your balance and fall over. This would leave you in an extremely vulnerable position and make it harder for you to fight back.

Moving back not only prevents these possibilities but also gets you closer to carrying out your own attack.

So, what should your attack be?

This can also be found in Si Nim Tau, however, unlike the other moves described earlier, this is found at the end of every section of Si Nim Tau. This is known as the elbow punch, referred to in the Si Nim Tau section as 'bring hands back'.

However, rather than just bringing your hands back, the motion is done with a lot of thrust to truly hurt anyone behind you at the time of this counterattack. Keep in mind that the opponent must be very close to you to be able to feel the maximum impact of the hit. When stepping back you would have to get as close as possible to them, facing away from them, and then do the elbow punch.

This can be done with both hands or with just one hand depending on the situation you are in. If you were to be pulled either left or right, then only one elbow would be able to make an impact and you would only have to do this move with one arm. Your arms would go from in front of you to by your side, with your elbows jutting out behind you, like this:

If you can turn around moving backwards, then I would recommend doing so as this would allow you to use a variety of punches as well as be able to see your opponent. However, if you are in a situation where you are unable to rotate to face your opponent, carrying out this move would still be effective.

The combined shock of both losing control of the pull and being repeatedly hit on their abdomen will force the attacker to back off.

Practise this technique with a friendly opponent a few times to make sure you begin to train your mind and arms to react in the right way.

7. Defending when grabbed from behind

An attacker may sometimes catch you by surprise when approaching you from behind. This is often also the case when they are part of a group. This attack may be aimed at restraining you while another person attacks. This may even happen at a party where there is a large crowd of people surrounding you and someone suddenly grabs you from behind without your consent.

When an attacker's arms are wrapped around your waist or chest, it is often very difficult to force yourself out of this position. Now, there are two possibilities here based on how you are being held. Either your arms are also trapped next to your body with their arms around you, or your arms are on the outside of their arms and free to move around.

If your hands are free to move around, which is usually more likely, you should execute the elbow punches mentioned earlier. This time, however, you will not have to step backwards to be able to perform this, as the attacker will already be right behind you ready to receive the blow to their solar plexus. If they refuse to let go, then your role is to continuously repeat the elbow punches until the pain they are in is unbearable and their body forces them to let go.

Sometimes the attacker may grab you in such a way that their arms are blocking your elbows from hitting their upper body. So, what would you do in this case? Well, you would do something remarkably similar to elbow punches. However, this time you would not use them by your side. Instead, you would lift your arms upwards in the same position by 90 degrees to your side (so that it may look like you have wings for arms), sticking out of your body. Here, you would have to twist your body as fast as you can in such a manner that you are aiming to hit the person grabbing you from behind in their face with your elbows from either side. Instinctively, as they move one way to dodge an elbow, if you rapidly throw an elbow from the other side, then they would move straight into your next attack. Also, if you do not manage to hit them, the repetitive twisting motion will make them slowly move backwards and loosen their grip and let go as they try to prevent themselves from being hit.

If the attacker has grabbed you and your hands are stuck next to you, you would not be able to bend your arms. Without being able to bend your arms, you would not be able to perform an elbow punch, so that option is no longer viable. So, what would you do?

The move you need to know for this scenario is called reverse 'Gum Sau', meaning 'pressing hand'. In the beginning of Section 4 of Si Nim Tau, I refer to it as a 'press[ing] hand'. In Si Nim Tau, this movement is done by both your hands, in front and then behind the body. The hand attacks with the palms tilted backwards so the base of the hand is what is really being used to hit, channelling the full force of the radius bone (the lower arm bone). For this scenario, you would use Gum Sau behind your body.

Similar to the elbow punch, you could choose to do this with only one hand, and in this case, this is what you would do. Firstly though, to be able to do the Gum Sau, you would need to give yourself a bit of space. This is because if your hands are trapped in front of you, you would not be able to move them behind you without having a bit of space. To create space for your move, all you would have to do is move your hips sideways, pushing their arm outwards, thus leaving more space for yourself. For the sake of the explanation, let us say that you have thrust your hips towards the left-hand side, giving yourself a bit of space to your right. Not only do you give yourself space, this also uncovers part of their body, including the groin. From here, your right hand would do a backwards Gum Sau into the groin, leaving the assaulter in unfathomable pain.

It would look like this (except with only one hand):

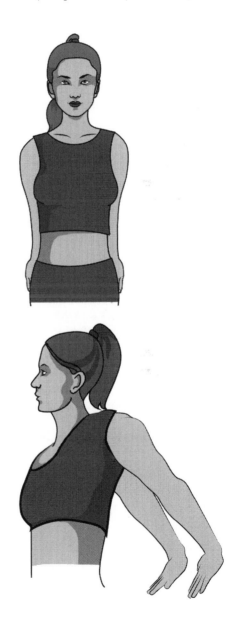

If they do not let go the first time, you could do this multiple times, as the pain would be unbearable. This would force them to let go and give you an opportunity to counterattack.

There is another move available to defend against this attack when your hands are pinned against you. It is one of my personal favourites because it is both counterintuitive and efficient. In this move, you relax your whole body and sink into the attacker's arms. However, make sure you do not lose your balance and fall since this would leave you extremely vulnerable to other attacks. The attacker's immediate response to having to carry your entire body weight would be to loosen or leave their grip, giving you the crucial moments required to counterattack.

Practise these techniques with the different forms of attacks with a friendly opponent a few times to make sure you begin to train your body to react and move in the right way.

8. Defending when lifted from behind

An attacker may sometimes catch you by surprise when approaching you from behind and not just grab you but also attempt to lift your body into the air.

Being lifted in the air is one of the worst possible positions anyone can be stuck in. If you are lifted in the air, you would have no control over your body and you would be in a very unbalanced, vulnerable position.

If you are lifted, similar to the techniques above, you could attempt to repeatedly use elbow punches at their face. However, when you are not grounded, it is exceedingly difficult to generate enough power for this to be fully effective. For this reason, it is best to attempt not to be lifted in the first place, and that is exactly what this defence technique is about.

In order not to be lifted, what you need to do is quite simple – wrap your foot around their foot.

You would do this from the inside of their legs and move your foot around their ankle to get a better grip. This makes it so that your attacker is now not just lifting your weight but also their own weight off the ground, which is impossible as it would defy the laws of gravity.

At first, such a simple technique may seem too good to be true; this is what I thought at first too.

I've tried this technique with a fellow student in my Kung Fu sessions. The person I practised this with is an extremely strong person and double my size. He would usually have no difficulty lifting me. However, when I used this method, he was simply unable to lift me, regardless of how much he tried. He too was in utter shock at what he experienced and eventually got fatigued from trying and let go.

Practise this technique with a friendly opponent, ideally someone a lot stronger and bigger than you, a few times to understand how easy and effective this move is and to familiarise yourself with the angle of the footlock to be used.

BRINGING IT ALL TOGETHER

Let's now continue the scenario we started with at the beginning of the book, "Just another night".

That is when he grabs you tightly by the shoulder and pushes you into a wall by your side, your head colliding painfully against it, leaving you dazed for a few fleeting seconds and unable to comprehend what he is muttering. The smell of alcohol now lingers in the air around you, storming aside everything pleasant previously felt. He is clearly intoxicated and not thinking straight but evidently stronger than you. At that very moment, you notice his hand reach out towards you.

He pulls his arm back and swings it wildly towards your face, planning to knock you out. You can hear his fist flying through the wind towards your cheek. However, you have practised this scenario multiple times already. You know what to expect, and you know how to stop it. You throw your arm at his bicep in the form of a Fook Sau and immediately stop his once powerful surging arm. With your free arm, you throw a straight punch at his nose. You hear a crack and some profanity muttered from the very shocked man.

Not having learned his lesson, he decides to throw a different type of punch, this time directed towards your ribs. Once again, you are confident of what to do and use a Gaun Sau, sweeping his hand away from your body and throwing him off balance for a few seconds. You once again throw a couple of rapid straight punches at his nose, leading to a few drops of blood finding their way out of his nostrils. Regardless of his fractured nose and eyes welling up with tears, he attempts to grab your hand to prevent you from using your Kung Fu again. However, you see this coming too. Now traumatised by your previous counterattacks, he is moving slower than before, and you immediately move the hand he is attempting to grab backwards and hit his arms away with your other hand.

As he stumbles, you throw a few more consecutive punches but this time aimed at his throat, cutting off all air from his lungs for a brief period. The man collapses on the spot, clutching at his throat and gasping for air.

You run out of the alleyway and into a more open road, pulling out your phone from your pocket and letting someone know what just happened to you so that they can confirm your safety.

Learning those few moves and practising them really paid off.

You must practise the techniques mentioned in this book with someone to help you understand how they work and figure out what works best for you. As my *sifus* (Kung Fu teachers) say, "You would never use a technique you're not comfortable with on the streets." Practising these techniques will help engrain them into your natural reflexes. Eventually, your confidence in your ability to stay calm and defend yourself will become your 'secret ingredient'.

Best of luck and stay safe.

ABOUT THE AUTHOR

Vedant J Maheshwari was born in Mumbai, India, in 2006 and moved to London at the age of two. He still spends most of his summers with his grandparents in India, who have had an immense influence on him.

Vedant goes to King's College School in London and has picked up multiple academic awards throughout his time there. He has been learning Kung Fu since the age of 11 and is currently an assistant instructor volunteering to teach young boys and girls Kung Fu over the weekend. In his free time, he enjoys practising squash, skiing and table tennis. He is a multilinguist with a working knowledge of five languages. He has completed the Duke of Edinburgh Bronze expedition.

Vedant enjoys travel with his parents. His favourite travel memories are from his eight-day Machu Picchu trek, an expedition of the Amazon Rainforest, a road trip through the deserts of Namibia and witnessing the Aurora Borealis.

Vedant believes that "Vincit qui se vincit," which translates from Latin to "He who conquers himself, conquers."

You can reach him through www.vedantjm.com or @VedantJM on Instagram.

ABOUT THE BOOK

This book has been created as a public service. Vedant is not earning any money from this book.

Proceeds from this book are going to Beder, a charity raising awareness around mental health and suicide prevention.

More information on Beder can be found at
www.beder.org.uk

NOTES

NOTES

NOTES